This book belongs to:

_____

# Celebrating Holidays in Hawai'i

by *Leslie Ann Hayashi*
*Illustrated by* Kathleen Wong Bishop

MUTUAL PUBLISHING

# Dedication

*To Mrs. "J" and all 4-H Leaders:*

Thank you for your generosity, guidance, and
encouragement "to make the best better."

*Leslie*

For Sri Eknath Easwaran who taught me
about the unity of life and that all people are One.

*Kathy*

Library of Congress Cataloging-in-Publication Data

Hayashi, Leslie Ann.
Celebrating holidays in Hawai'i / by Leslie Ann Hayashi ; illustrated by Kathleen Wong Bishop.
p. cm. -- (Let's celebrate!)
ISBN 1-56647-914-2 (hardcover : alk. paper)
1. Holidays--Hawaii--Juvenile literature. I. Bishop, Kathleen Wong, ill. II. Title.
GT4810.H3H39 2009
394.269969--dc22
2009027752

**Editor's Note:** All crafts and cooking activities
should be supervised by an adult.

ISBN-10: 1-56647-914-2
ISBN-13: 978-1-56647-914-1

First Printing, August 2010

Mutual Publishing, LLC
1215 Center Street, Suite 210
Honolulu, Hawai'i 96816
Ph: 808-732-1709 / Fax: 808-734-4094
Email: info@mutualpublishing.com
www.mutualpublishing.com

Printed in Taiwan

# Let's Celebrate!

Hawai'i is home to many cultural traditions. There's something for kama'āina (residents) and malahini (visitors) alike. Come join us in celebrating our state's special holidays!

# JAPANESE NEW YEAR
## January 1

Unlike other Asian countries, Japan celebrates the New Year on January 1. Special foods are served. *O-zoni* is a soup with mochi dumplings representing prosperity. *Sashimi,* or raw fish, represents good luck, while *mochi* made from rice represents long life. The *kadomatsu,* an arrangement of pine, bamboo, and plum blossoms, literally means "gates of pine." Placed near the door, it symbolizes longevity, prosperity, and strength.

All day long grandfather pounds
the *mochi* inside an *usu,* a stone mortar.
Watch out for the wooden splinters!

# Peanut Butter Mochi

1 cup peanut butter, 1/4 cup honey, 3 cups water,
1 cup sugar, 16 ounces of mochiko flour, potato starch

Combine peanut butter and honey for filling. Refrigerate a few hours. Boil water. Add sugar and stir until dissolved. Gradually add mochiko flour. Stir constantly over medium heat until lumps are dissolved. Spread potato starch on a surface and roll dough. Cool slightly. Sprinkle more potato starch and knead a few times until smooth. Form 2 (12-inch -long) pieces. Cut an inch of dough and flatten into a circle. Place a teaspoon of filling in the center. Fold edges around filling and pinch to seal. Makes 2 dozen.

Kadomatsu
"Gates of Pine"

O-zoni
Prosperity

Sashimi
Good Luck

Mochi
Long Life

# Chinese New Year
## Mid-January to Mid-February

Chinese New Year falls on the first day of the first month of the new lunar year. A different animal of the zodiac represents each year: rat, ox, tiger, rabbit, dragon, snake, horse, sheep, monkey, rooster, dog, and boar. Good wishes are written on red posters in calligraphy while firecrackers scare away bad spirits. Lucky money is given in red envelopes called *li-see*. *Gau,* a traditional sweet treat, is served. Its round shape and stickiness represent family unity.

See the lion dance! We feed him our *li-see* for good luck. Gung Hee Fat Choy!

## Microwave Gau

1 pound Chinese brown sugar (cake type),
2 cups hot water, 16 ounces box mochiko flour,
12 ounces can coconut milk, 1/4 cup salad oil,
sesame seeds, red dates

Dissolve cake sugar in boiling water. Cool.
Stir in mochiko gradually to make a thin batter.
Stir in coconut milk and oil; beat until smooth.
Grease microwave bundt pan. Pour into pan.
Cook on high for 16 minutes. Let stand
10 minutes. Sprinkle with sesame
seeds and top with red dates.

# TET NGUYEN DAN
## Vietnamese New Year
## Mid-January to Mid-February

Vietnamese New Year, or Tet Nguyen Dan, means the first morning of the first day of the new year. During the week-long celebration, families exchange gifts. Everyone receives new clothes and shoes. Homes are cleaned to get rid of bad fortune, and debts are paid. Family and friends resolve their disagreements. A week before Tet, the Kitchen Gods leave to visit the Jade Emperor in the heaven court. They report on the family's events during the past year. This day is known as the Feast of the Kitchen Gods, or Le Tao Quan.

## Make a Noisemaker

Place dried beans inside a foil pie pan.
Cut crêpe paper streamers and tape on the inside.
Place another pie pan on top of the other.
Tape pie pans together.

Quick! Cover your ears. At midnight, firecrackers, gongs, and other noise makers usher out the old to make way for the new.

On New Year's Eve the family altar is decorated with lanterns and flowers. At midnight a special ceremony called Le Tru Tich is held. Firecrackers, gongs, and other noisy items usher out the old and make way for the new.

# Portuguese Malasada Day
## February/March

Portuguese laborers from the Azores first came to work on Hawai'i's plantations in 1878. They brought a fried pastry called the malasada. Using all their butter and sugar, they made large batches of malasadas. Malasada Day is celebrated on Fat Tuesday (also known as Shrove Tuesday). It's the Tuesday before Ash Wednesday, the first day of Lent, forty days before Easter.

After the malasadas are cooked,
Aunty Rose rolls them in sugar and hands them to us.
Mmmm. Every day should be Malasada Day!

## Easy Malasadas

1 cup milk, 1 egg, ½ teaspoon of lemon extract,
2 cups of Bisquick, 5 slices of white bread, oil, sugar

Combine milk, egg, and lemon extract.
Stir in Bisquick. Cut the white bread into quarters.
Dip bread into the batter and fry in hot oil (375° F).
Cook about 2 minutes or until golden brown.
Drain on paper towels. Roll in sugar.
Makes about 20 malasadas.

In addition to the malasada, the Portuguese brought with them the *cavaquinho,* a four-stringed instrument that became the 'ukulele, or "jumping flea."

Let's light the lanterns on the tiered stand.
Let's put peach blossoms on the tiered stand.
Five court musicians are playing flutes and drums.
Today is a happy Dolls' Festival.

*Akari wo tsukemasho bonbori ni*
*O hana wo agemasho momo no hana*
*Gonin bayashi no fue daiko*
*Kyou wa tanoshii hina matsuri.*

# Girl's Day
## March 3

Doll displays mark the beginning of Hina Matsuri or the Girl's Day Festival. Originally the dolls were made of paper. People believed that bad luck and illnesses could be transferred to these dolls and then thrown into a river or the sea. Now the dolls are treasured heirlooms. In addition to serving tea, girls also play *ojami*, a juggling game using beanbags, or *otedanna*. Parents pray for their young daughter's growth and happiness. They give peach blossoms in hopes of a peaceful life. This festival teaches discipline, patience, neatness, and responsibility.

*Ochagashi*
*Tea sweets*

Mariko and Sachi share tea and sweets.
*Hishi* mochi has three colors: white for purity, pink
for energy, and green for fertility.

## Make the Dairi-Sama: Emperor and Empress

Draw two triangles on poster paper. Add circles on top for heads. Draw two faces.
Emperor: Draw a small oval around his head for hair. Add a short horizontal line with
a long rectangle on top. Draw big sleeves with hands showing. Empress: Draw a big
oval around her head for hair. Add a small circle with three pointed rectangles for
a crown. Draw little sleeves with hands. Add a half circle above her hands for a fan.
Draw lines on the fan. Color their clothes with bright colors and patterns.

Girl's Day is also known
as Hina Matsuri, or Doll
Festival. The Emperor and
Empress preside over the
Girl's Day display of dolls.
Below are five to seven
tiers with other members
of the imperial court. The
fifteen cloth and porcelain
dolls include court ladies,
musicians, ministers,
and deputy chiefs. The
display also features small
trays of *mochi* and other
household items.

Come swim and picnic at Kūhiō Beach Park in honor of the prince!

# Prince Kūhiō Day
## March 26

Prince Kūhiō Day celebrates the birthday of the "citizen prince." He was born on March 26, 1871. After his father died, Jonah Kūhiō Kalanianaʻole was adopted by his uncle David Kalākaua. Later, when Kalākaua was elected king, Jonah became a prince. In 1902 Kūhiō was elected Hawaiʻi's delegate to Congress. He served twenty years until his death on January 7, 1922. During his terms, he introduced a statehood bill and worked to establish Hawaiian homestead lands. In 1940 his home in Waikīkī was given to the City of Honolulu and officially dedicated as Kūhiō Beach Park. Today his birthday is a state holiday.

# Haupia

1/3 cup sugar, 6 tablespoons cornstarch,
3/4 cup water, 1 ½ cups coconut milk

In a saucepan combine sugar and cornstarch.
Stir in water and blend well. Add coconut milk.
Cook and stir over low heat until thickened.
Pour into an 8 x 8-inch pan and chill until firm.
Cut into 2-inch squares.

Lūʻau
Hawaiian Feast

Kālua Pig

Poi

Lomi-Lomi
Salmon

Haupia

HAPPY BIRTHDAY PRINCE KŪHIŌ!

# EARTH DAY
## April 22

Long before Earth Day was created, ancient Hawaiians respected and cared for the 'āina, or land. In 1969 at a United Nations Conference on the Environment, John McConnell introduced the idea of celebrating the earth on a specific day. Two years later the United Nations issued this proclamation:

> May there only be peaceful and cheerful Earth days to come for our beautiful Spaceship Earth as it continues to spin and circle in frigid space with its warm and fragile cargo of animate life.

> -UN Secretary-General U Thant, February 26, 1971, United Nations Earth Day

On March 21, 1970, San Francisco Mayor Joseph Alioto issued one of the first Earth Day proclamations. U.S. Senator Gaylord Nelson of Wisconsin promoted Earth Day in the United States. Today more than five hundred million people in almost two hundred countries participate in Earth Day. It is a time to celebrate and cherish the beautiful planet we call home.

# LEARN DIFFERENT WAYS
# YOU CAN HELP OUR EARTH

Cleaning streams and beaches protects our oceans.

Planting native shrubs, flowers, and trees is a good way to honor our 'āina.

RECYCLE

Recycling helps our environment.

Come watch the Lei Day parade. But look out for the pooper scoopers!

# Lei Day
## May 1

Writer Don Blanding wanted to promote the enchanting Hawaiian tradition of making lei. Grace Tower Warren suggested the celebration occur in conjunction with May Day. She coined the phrase, "May Day is Lei Day." Leonard and Ruth Hawk wrote the lyrics and composed the music to the popular song, "May Day is Lei Day in Hawai'i." The first Lei Day was held in Honolulu on May 1, 1928. It included lei-making demonstrations, exhibits, and contests along with hula and music. The next year, Lei Day became an official holiday in the territory, interrupted only during World War II. Every year the lei queen title alternates among three generations; a young woman, a mature woman, and a grandmother.

## Make a Lei

Cut flowers from bright paper.
Punch holes in the flowers' middles.
Cut drinking straws into 1" pieces.
Cut 36" yarn.
Tape the end of the yarn to sew with it.
Sew flowers and straws together, alternating.
Tie together.

### May Day is Lei Day

*May Day is Lei Day in Hawai'i*
*Garlands of flowers everywhere*
*All of the colors in the rainbow*
*Maidens with blossoms in their hair*

*Flowers that mean we should be happy*
*Throwing aside a load of care*
*Oh, May Day is Lei Day in Hawai'i*
*May Day is happy days out there.*

- Lyrics and music by
Leonard and Ruth Hawk

# Boy's Day
## May 5

Boy's Day is also known as Tango-no-sekku, or Festival of the Horse. Male dolls and *koi nobori,* or carp streamers, are displayed. The fish streamers are made of paper or cloth and are attached to poles. The carp's sizes reflect the boys' ages: the older the boy, the larger the carp. Like the noble koi, parents hope their sons will grow to be brave and strong. Dolls of warriors, knights, and martial arts figures protect the boys from evil and teach them manliness. Momotaro, the Peach Boy, and Benkei, a warrior priest, also inspire boys to overcome life's challenges. Japan no longer celebrates separate Boy's and Girl's Days; instead Children's Day is celebrated on May 5.

## Make a Carp Streamer

Fold construction paper
in half lengthwise.
Draw the outline of half a fish
and cut it out to form a whole fish.

Cut fins from different colored paper:
one top fin and two lower fins.
Glue onto the fish.
Draw stripes on the tail.

Cut out scales from many colors.
Make some scales with foil.
Glue the scales onto the fish in
overlapping rows.
Add an eye made from silver foil.

Kenji and Yoshi fly their carp streamers.
Legend says the carp was so strong and brave
it traveled up waterfalls and swam into the
heavens, where it became a dragon.

# Father's Day
## Third Sunday in June

Adult children wishing to honor their parents led to the creation of Father's and Mother's Day. After her mother died, Mrs. Sonora Smart Dodd and her five siblings were raised by her father. Mrs. Dodd started the first Father's Day, celebrated on June 19, 1910, almost one hundred years ago. In 1972 Father's Day was made a national holiday.

# Mother's Day
## Second Sunday in May

Miss Anna Jarvas wished to honor her mother, who raised eleven children. Mother's Day was first celebrated in May 1914. President Woodrow Wilson proclaimed the second Sunday in May as the official Mother's Day.

In Hawai'i, ohana, or family, is very important.

# Grandparents Day

## First Sunday in September after Labor Day

Marian McQuade of West Virginia founded Grandparents Day. In 1978 Congress proclaimed the first Sunday after Labor Day as Grandparents Day. President Jimmy Carter signed the proclamation " ... to honor grandparents … and to help children become aware of the strength, information, and guidance older people can offer." In Hawai'i, families extend beyond blood ties with the practice of hānai, or informal adoption.

emery

## Hand Prints

Pour non-toxic paint into a shallow pan.
Place hands in paint and press onto paper.
Write a message for Mom, Dad, or Grandparents.
Sign your name, and write your age and the date.

# King Kamehameha I Day
## June 11

King Kamehameha I Day celebrates the birthday of Kamehameha I, who was born between 1752 and 1761. In 1810, after twenty years, he united the islands of Kaua'i, Maui, Moloka'i, Lāna'i, O'ahu, and Hawai'i, the Big Island. During the twenty-year period, he fought many famous battles between long periods of peace. King Kamehameha died in May 1819. His burial place remains unknown. However, many believe his remains were taken to a secret cave along the Kona coast on the Island of Hawai'i. King Kamehameha's birthday is honored with a week-long celebration of music, hula, and lei. Families enjoy the parade and have picnics on this state holiday.

*Hawai'i Pono'ī*

*Hawai'i pono'ī,*
*Nānā i kou mō'ī,*
*Ka lani ali'i,*
*Ke ali'i.*

***Hui:***
*Makua lani e,*
*Kamehameha e,*
*Nā kāua e pale*
*Me ka ihe.*

*Hawai'i's Own\**

Hawai'i's own,
Look to your king,
The royal chief,
The chief.

**Chorus:**
Royal father,
Kamehameha,
We will defend
With spears.

In 1874 King Kalākaua wrote "Hymn of Kamehameha I" to honor King Kamehameha. Royal Hawaiian Bandmaster Heinrich Berger arranged the music. The song later became known as "Hawai'i Pono'ī." It was Berger's favorite song, and he ended every concert with it. "Hawai'i Pono'ī." became the national anthem of the Kingdom of Hawai'i. In 1967 Hawai'i's state legislature proclaimed "Hawai'i Pono'ī." the state anthem. Today it is played at many public events.

\*Sheet music from Paul Kahn Collection, Hawai'i State Archives.

The King Kamehameha statue is decorated with long colorful strands of lei.

# OBON
## Summer

Obon is a Japanese Buddhist event honoring ancestors. This Feast of the
Dead is similar to All Souls Day. During this time, folk or bon dances are
performed. In the 1930s Japanese immigrants on Hawaiʻi's plantations
organized bon dances. They chose different weekends to celebrate. That is
why the bon season stretches over the summer unlike in Japan, where it is
celebrated for only three days. Dancers wear full-length kimonos, yukata,
a light cotton garment, or the half-length kimono known as the happi coat.
Beginners come in rubber slippers and shorts! In Hawaiʻi, people also go
to the Obon festival to buy their favorite foods—beef teriyaki sticks, saimin,
corn on the cob, and more.

During the bon season, ancestors return to earth. Floating lanterns are also released into the ocean to guide the spirits back to their world on the last day of the season. This tradition is now embraced by people of all faiths.

## Make a Floating Lantern

Cut ½ gallon milk carton, leaving 4 inches on the bottom. Cut out squares on each side. On tissue paper write a prayer to honor an ancestor. Tape inside on the openings. Tape a tea candle on the bottom.

*Tanko Bushi*

*Tsuki ga deta deta tsuki ga deta*      Here comes the moon,
*Uchi no oyama no ueni deta*      Over our mountain.
*Anmari entotsu ga takai node*      Is the chimney too high?
*Sazoya otsukisama kemutakaro*      I wonder if smoke stings the moon.
*Sano yoi yoi*      Ah, ah.

This popular bon dance song is performed at most dances. The shoveling movements are easy to learn.

# Dragon Boat Festival
## June/July

The Dragon Boat Race festival may have started as ancient worship of the river dragon or in memory of the famous Chinese poet, Qu Yuan. He was a scholar who served the King of Chu during China's great wars. Qu Yuan demanded government reforms, but the king refused. Discouraged, he threw himself into the Milo River in Hunan on the fifth day of the fifth month. People rushed to save him, but Qu Yuan drowned. Dragon boat races commemorate that attempt to save him. The team has twenty paddlers, a drummer, and a steer person. The first three rows of paddlers are the "pacers;" the middle rows are the "engine;" while the paddlers at the back are the "rockets" or "terminators." With everyone paddling together, the narrow boat flies over the water like an arrow.  In Hawai'i dragon boat races are held at Ala Moana Park in June or July. They are also popular worldwide.

## Make a Dragon Boat

Fold a paper in half. Draw a 4-inch x 4-inch dragon head with its nose on the fold. Cut the head out. Decorate both sides.

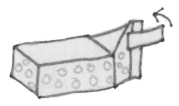

Open the spout of a quart-size milk carton and tape the edges together so the spout sticks out.

Cut a flap from the long side of the carton to make a tail. Don't cut the edge along the bottom of the carton.

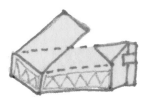

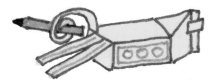

Cut the tail into 3 strips. Wrap each strip around a pencil to make it curl.

Cut small triangles along the top edges of the boat. Tape the dragon head to the spout.

# Admissions Day
## Third Friday in August

Hawai'i became the fiftieth state on August 21, 1959. Admissions Day, which marks that historic event, is a state holiday. Hawai'i's history is unique as it is the only state which was once a monarchy. King Kamehameha I was the first of nine rulers; there were seven other ruling kings and one ruling queen. In 1894 Hawai'i became a republic; six years later it became a territory. Alaska and Hawai'i competed to become the forty-nineth state; Alaska won by becoming a state on January 3, 1959.

### Hawai'i's Flag

The state flag was the same one used while Hawai'i was a kingdom from 1810 to 1893. King Kamehameha I requested a flag for the new country. It had eight stripes of white, red, and blue, representing the eight main islands. The flag of Great Britain was emblazoned in the upper left corner to honor Hawai'i's friendship with the British. The combination of the stripes of the United States' flag and the Union Jack of Great Britain pleased both nations.

### Make Hawai'i's State Flag

Copy and enlarge this flag on white paper. Color the areas red and blue like the flag on the pole.

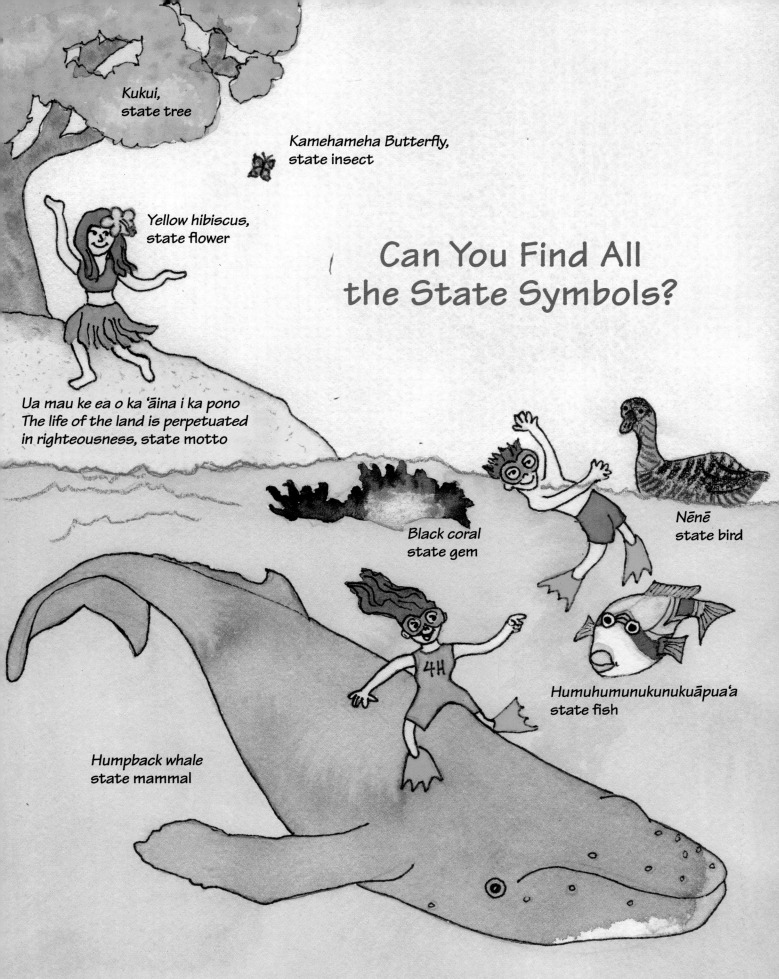

Kukui,
state tree

Kamehameha Butterfly,
state insect

Yellow hibiscus,
state flower

# Can You Find All the State Symbols?

Ua mau ke ea o ka 'āina i ka pono
The life of the land is perpetuated
in righteousness, state motto

Black coral
state gem

Nēnē
state bird

Humuhumunukunukuāpua'a
state fish

Humpback whale
state mammal

# CHUSOK, KOREAN AUTUMN NIGHT
## August 15

Chusok, or Korean Autumn Night, occurs on the brightest full moon which is the fifteenth night of the eighth month of the lunar calendar. It begins the harvest season and is known as the Korean Thanksgiving. Families gather and eat rice cakes called *song pyun,* which are made of rice, beans, sesame seeds, and chestnuts. Families visit ancestors' graves to offer rice and fruits. They clean the graves, watch the moon, and feast. Children, dressed in *hanbok,* traditional Korean clothing, play games and sing songs while everyone gives thanks for their blessings.

## Make a Moon Painting

Place a bowl upside down on a piece of paper.
Paint around the bowl.
Add stars to the night sky.

Come join us as we hold hands and dance under the bright moon.

Uncle Mario and I surprise Aunty Marcelina by making a beautiful parol.

# Christmas
## December 25

Christmas festivities in the Philippines are decorated with all sizes of *parols,* Filipino star-shaped lanterns with bright streamers. The word *parol* comes from farol, the Spanish word for lantern. These lanterns developed from the piñata, which came to the Philippines when Spaniards brought Christianity to the islands. Many Filipinos in Hawai'i continue this tradition. *Parols* can be made from bamboo, crêpe paper, rice paper, shells, coconuts, and candles. They have tassels, sometimes one on each point. Electric lights are now used instead of candles.

## Make a *Parol*: Filipino Star of Bethlehem

Recycle a round plastic lid to make the *parol*. On colored paper, draw two five-pointed stars to fit on the lid, one for each side. To draw a star start at number 1, draw a straight line to number 2, 3, and so on, ending at number 1. Cut the stars out and glue on the lid. Decorate the stars with glitter. Make 4 "tassels" for the points of the star. Snip about 4 times on one end of a small rectangle of paper. Glue the other end to a point on the *parol*. Make a hole in the plastic by the point without a tassel to hang the *parol* with a string.

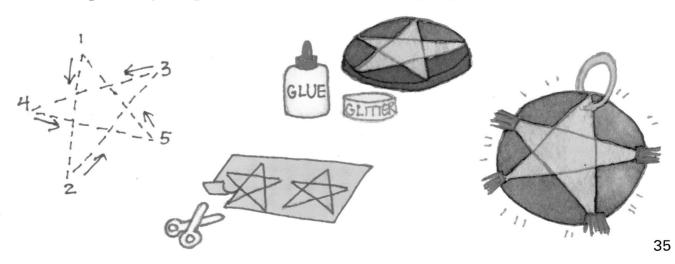

## Author & Illustrator

Friends since first grade, Leslie and Kathy joined 4-H when they were nine years old. They spent many fun hours learning to cook, bake, sew, create crafts, take photographs, and be good citizens and leaders.

Other Mutual books by Leslie and Kathy:

*Fables from the Deep*
*Fables Beneath the Rainbow*
*Aloha ʻOe*
*A Fishy Alphabet in Hawaiʻi*

Visit Leslie and Kathy at *www.Fablesfromthefriends.com*